50 Shades of Pray

50 Shades of Pray

Ken Stuczynski

Copyright © 2025 by Ken Stuczynski
All rights reserved. No part of this book may be reproduced in any manner whatsoever without written permission except in the case of brief quotations embodied in critical articles and reviews.
First Printing, 2025

Amorphous Publishing Guild
Buffalo, New York
www.Amorphous.Press

Cover Image by Venrike Artworks, from Pixabay

This book has no relation to any other book by the same title.

Contents

Introduction **viii**

1. Beginnings **1**
2. Promises **2**
3. Passages **3**
4. Repetition **4**
5. Posture **5**
6. Gestures **6**
7. Fasting **7**
8. Vigil **8**
9. Labor **9**

~ { V }

10 Pain **10**

11 Release **11**

12 Tradition **12**

13 Contemplation **13**

14 Study **14**

15 Bargaining **15**

16 Worship **16**

17 Adoration **17**

18 Thanksgiving **18**

19 Confession **19**

20 Consecration **20**

21 Objects **21**

22 Food & Drink **22**

23 Music & Song **23**

24 Dance **24**

25 Supplication **25**

26 Intercession **26**

{ VI } ~

27 Release **27**

28 Pilgrimage **28**

29 Retreat **29**

30 Silence **30**

31 Nature **31**

32 The Spirit **32**

33 Existential **33**

34 Charity **34**

35 Communal **35**

36 Anger **36**

37 Washing **37**

38 Physical Love **38**

39 Pride **39**

40 Parental **40**

41 Blessing **41**

42 Obligatory **42**

43 Resistance **43**

{ VII }

44 Notes **44**

45 Prayer List **45**

46 Outsourcing **46**

47 Without Ceasing **47**

48 ... **48**

49 ... **49**

50 ... **50**

About the Author **51**

Introduction

What is prayer?

In its essence, prayer is simply communing with G-d, the Divine Other. I say communing instead of communicating because the relationship you have with anyone isn't purely words. It is about sharing time and space together, to be in each other's presence.

Many best friends are content to just sit and be together. Much is spoken without a word; much is shared without a thought. It's about the time you spend and what you share, however enlightened or mundane, planned or spontaneous. As G-d is greater than any and all of us, the ways we can commune are more boundless than in our relationships with each other.

Find Your Prayer Fingerprint

There are many beliefs that certain ways of prayer are more or less proper. Some may even be forbidden by Man under the authority of this or that preacher. You need not worry about those forms of prayer if your conscience tells you to seek G-d in other ways. And not all forms of prayer or worship will resonate with you. We each have our own personality, our own way of being and communicating with others, so it's natural that G-d can reach and teach us according to the shape he has given to our particular soul both in birth and our life experiences. We each have a "prayer fingerprint".

This book is all about possibilities — exploring all the ways you can be and speak with G-d. There may be things you have never considered as "prayer" and things you've always done but never thought about. Some of these will feel natural and others will be awkward, or even challenging. You may have existing prayer habits you want to build on, and others you want to try for the first time. You may be an introvert who appreciates stillness, or an extrovert who longs for uplifted voices and the breaking of bread.

You are a unique creation. The way you pray reflects your unique personal relationship with G-d and no one else's. Your voice and silence, sadness and joy, passions and fears, are all uniquely yours. You can acknowledge them all before G-d, and it may surprise and transform you when you do.

Never Stop Growing

Your prayer fingerprint won't always be the same. It might be different before and after exploring this book. People grow and change, and their relationship with G-d grows and changes, and that is as it should be. The challenges of life aren't put there by accident. They may force us to let go of some things and discover others. There will always be ways, even in the darkest of times and places, where we can connect and commune with G-d. If we openly share all our experiences with G-d, we will never be alone, and the Light will shine through us to those we Love, and to the world.

About Writing This Book

The original idea for this book was much more extensive, but the author felt a more concise pocketbook would be best. Perhaps an expanded book on prayer is forthcoming. If you are inspired by this small work, please let the author know. And let him know what other forms of prayer you added to the list! His information can be found at the back of this book.

{ 1 }

Beginnings

There is an old expression that no one "should ever engage in any important undertaking without first invoking the aid and blessing of Deity".

The beginning of a journey, or a game, or a marriage, or even a meeting, can be blessed if we would only think to ask. What better way to mark the beginning of anything meaningful in life than to take that moment and share it with G-d.

{ 2 }

Promises

We've all heard the phrase, "So help me G-d". Maybe you don't believe in swearing oaths. But we all ought to do what we say we will do.

If you get into any promise, contract, or other obligation, keep G-d in mind. Ask for the wisdom to know you are doing the right thing. Ask for the strength to carry it out. Every bond you make with someone, especially with G-d, becomes part of your life. Making it mindfully in the Divine presence adds a solid spiritual foundation to those relationships. Recalling your duties thereafter reminds you of your duty to G-d.

{ 3 }

Passages

What if G-d could say the right thing to you at the right time? There are passages in scripture, as well as other works, that may fit nearly any occasion or mood. The breadth of G-d's voice is boundless, and these words can become love letters for you to revisit when you need them. Just as you can hear a person's voice in a thoughtful hand-scribbled note, whispers of the Divine can be heard by your soul.

Seek out these passages. Bookmark them. Print them off and post them. Read them as often as you like, and hear them as G-d whispering to your soul. Let it touch your thoughts and heart here and now.

{ 4 }

Repetition

Litanies, rosaries, prayer beads, mantras ... repetitive prayer is a unique form of communing with G-d. When the conscious mind is focused and keeps focusing, distractions fade away. It may feel like you've exhausted your thoughts, and that sets your conscious mind aside to let the message sink in. It can even end in a silence that lets you hear a Divine Whisper.

Any message, phrase, or even a single word can be used. You can devote the words to pray about a particular person or thing. When done regularly, it's like a path in the woods broadened by your footsteps every time you travel it.

{ 5 }

Posture

Our posture can make us attentive or relaxed, receptive or closed. And there have always been postures associated with prayer. It is natural at times to lift up your arms or fall on your knees. Clasping or pressing your hands together, or bowing your head, evokes a mindset of humility.

You may have been taught a posture or you can purposely choose one. If you associate a posture with prayer, it can place you immediately in a prayerful mindset. When you sit or stand or have your hands a certain way, you know you are setting aside that time for G-d.

{ 6 }

Gestures

Like a hand on the shoulder, or waving to a friend, a gesture is worth a thousand words. Some bow or genuflect to express respect, or extend their hand toward whom they are praying for. Such simple actions become a shorthand message to G-d that you are actively directing your attention in prayer.

You might trace a cross with your thumb in the palm of your other hand when you hear a siren, thinking of those in need and those caring for them. It can be a subtle thing no one will notice. It takes only a moment. Whatever gesture you associate with prayer, make it a part of your regular connection to G-d.

Fasting

Fasting is not going on a diet. It may be done as a sacrifice, but it's about self-denial and humility. It makes your body send a signal that something has changed and needs attention. This is a way of placing yourself in a position of need before G-d, not just in your heart, but your body as well. When done safely, fasting could mean not eating certain things, or only eating after sundown for a month, or only drinking water for a day or more. It should always be done safely, according to your health and lifestyle.

Fasting makes you more aware of your needs and desires. Fasting puts them in perspective, and makes room for attention to G-d.

… # { 8 }

Vigil

A religious service the day before a holy day is often called a vigil. But keeping vigil (or "keeping watch") is merely a pause from sleep for prayerfulness. Like fasting is about the body, fasting from sleep is about giving up or setting aside time. Unlike the time you spend for work or play, a vigil is truly about putting aside the things of the world.

It could be a whole night or part of a night. It could be spent in other forms of prayer. Or you could do other activities, so long as you offer them to G-d, and as time spent in quiet Divine presence.

{ 9 }

Labor

We may dedicate ourselves to a profession or a cause, but the effort itself can be done in prayerfulness. It could be any task, from weeding a garden to painting a fence, from crunching numbers to writing a book. Lifting up one's labors is a way of elevating what you are doing right here and now. You are placing yourself, through your actions, before the Divine Presence. Let G-d be your company in such things. There is no need to leave G-d behind as if you only have time when you rest.

Does not G-d wish to be with you in your busiest moments? Don't imagine it to be an imposition or distraction, but gratefulness for the company of a loved one in the workplace.

{ 10 }

Pain

Offering up your pain to G-d isn't a spiritual way of "walking it off". It's not about asking for the pain to go away, or having someone to take on the pain for you. It's not even about comfort. G-d created you and a world where pain was possible, and shares in all our experiences, even the unpleasant ones. G-d lives in the World through us. G-d feels everything we feel, including pain.

The willful acceptance of pain is a gift. In offering up our pain, we are showing G-d that we accept all the experiences of Creation, and his plan for us. And in acknowledging G-d's place in sharing such experiences, all things become bearable and a blessing.

{ 11 }

Release

What does it mean to "Let Go, Let G-d"? Imagine if we asked a parent to fix a toy, but when we handed it to them, we didn't let go. It seems silly, but most of us do not have the trust of a child. Or we take self-reliance and personal responsibility to the point where there's no room of G-d in our journey. We even want to control the universe and other people

Worrying is also not letting go. Look to the Divine Parent with the trust of a child. Don't just pray for something out of your control to line up or work out. Consciously let go. Recognize the problem is out of your hands. To the extent you can make peace with doing that is the reach of your faith.

{ 12 }

Tradition

Most of us pray how we were taught as a child -- grace before meals, going to weekly services, or praying before going to sleep. Maybe we were not taught at all. Sometimes we pray because of habit, or it's expected of us by others. But human beings need tradition. There is not a culture in existence without its holidays and rituals. So why not embrace those traditions that honor G-d?

Look at the traditions you already follow. Which ones bring you closer to G-d? What if you stopped doing them? What if you did other traditions differently so that G-d was part of it? It's never too late to start a tradition, for yourself and those close to you.

{ 13 }

Contemplation

Contemplation is rolling over in one's mind some idea or thing. It could be pondering the mysteries of life or the beauty of nature. Why not include G-d in this inner dialogue? You could even make the Divine the subject of your contemplation. To make this prayerful, all you need to do is open the door to thoughts and feelings from G-d. This makes the source of inspiration greater than yourself.

{ 14 }

Study

When studying scripture or other inspired works, context matters. What did the writer mean? What does it mean objectively, if anything? Or you can ask yourself how it speaks to you, right here and now. When you focus on the Divine message behind inspired words, that last question is the most prayerful.

Learning about scripture can give you a deeper understanding of it. Reading other people's commentaries can give you new ideas about it. But you don't have to be a scholar to connect intimately with G-d through scripture. There is a reward just from devoting time to reading from where you are in your own life.

{ 15 }

Bargaining

How can anyone really bargain with G-d? Yet we hear of times where someone says they will do or sacrifice something if G-d gives them victory in battle or some other benefit. If we do this, we might be trying to bribe G-d. Maybe we are testing G-d. Divine Love is unconditional, but ours is not. We may think of G-d as limited as ourselves.

Or maybe it's a way to set ourselves straight to feel we deserve Grace. We say that if we get what we want or need, we will acknowledge G-d's hand in it. We will dedicate our life going forward, even transform ourselves as an act of thanks. It's part of our conversation with G-d about the future.

{ 16 }

Worship

Worship is not just adoration or other forms of prayer. It may be done as a group or even alone. It may mean putting on certain clothes, going to a certain place, or doing some ritual or tradition.

Worship is consciously setting aside a time and place devoted to such things, and nothing else. It's like a festival of prayerful activities, structured and formal, or spontaneous and free-flowing. It's about creating a sacred, safe space to openly acknowledge G-d.

{ 17 }

Adoration

Have you ever thought about someone and just adored them? It could be a loved one or a celebrity. It's a feeling of veneration and respect for who they are. Surely G-d is worthy of it. Why not take some time just to place yourself in the Divine Presence in a posture of true appreciation. Recall everything that G-d is. Recall all G-d has done, and does forevermore.

{ 18 }

Thanksgiving

Adoration and praise are about what G-d is and has done. Thanksgiving is more personal. You thank someone because of something they did for you that had an impact on your life.

Count your blessings. There are so many reasons to be grateful. If you truly appreciate them, why wouldn't you thank the Giver of all good things? Why only pray for what you do not have? If your prayers are answered, is that all? Thanksgiving brings you back and deepens your appreciation and acknowledgment of G-d.

{ 19 }

Confession

Baring your soul makes you feel vulnerable. Sometimes you need to feel that -- confessing to another -- as way to come to grips with your own failings. Who is safer to open up to than G-d? Who is best to help you forgive yourself?

And yet we fear judgment. We may have guilt and shame. But these things can't be kept to yourself, nor should you want to. G-d doesn't need your confession, you do. Nothing is unknown or secret, after all. But it's a way to take deep, personal responsibility. It can set you free, or rather let's G-d raise you from the weight of your imperfect self.

{ 20 }

Consecration

Making a place holy means setting it apart for devotion. The very act of such consecration is a prayer, and is often done as a group with ritual and tradition. But it doesn't have to be a physical place.

You can dedicate a certain day, or time of day, to prayer. Like you may dedicate a building in someone's name, you can dedicate a place to G-d's will. It could be a place of healing, or education, or art, or even your own home. And it can be done mindfully whenever you enter that place -- a threshold prayer. You may even mark such an entrance-way with a symbol that speaks to your faith, reminding you of Divine Presence.

{ 21 }

Objects

Anything with spiritual significance to you can be a tool for prayer. It could be a framed poem or scripture passage. It could be an image of a blessed person or event, or even a symbol of your faith. It could be a piece of jewelry or something you keep in your pocket.

Such things can be a focus of prayer. They can be an ever-present reminder. And when you employ something that is always there, it lingers in the back of your mind, even when you are doing something else, somewhere else.

{ 22 }

Food & Drink

Eating and drinking are basic human activities. Maybe we don't give them much thought. Maybe we think consuming sustenance is a base pleasure at best. But that's no reason not to be mindful of G-d in the midst of such things.

We can be thankful to have our needs met, or to enjoy a good meal or beverage. But why not mindfully dedicate the experience? Why not share it with G-d as you might with family or a close friend? Every meal, every dish, every glass, is an opportunity to place yourself in a unique way in G-d's presence.

{ 23 }

Music & Song

Few things touch the heart like Music. It makes us feel. It excites us, or soothes our mood, or reminds us of a memory or idea. Listening is meditative. It lets our minds wander in contemplation.

Chanting and instruments have been found in worship since the beginning. Prayers have been set to music. There is a saying,"He who sings prays twice". Being part of the music elevates the sense of presence. Almost any music can be employed for such things. As you may listen for G-d in nature, why not in song? Surely we can find much inspired from above.

{ 24 }

Dance

Like Music, dance can be used to express ourselves. Unlike music alone, dance makes us move!

Sometimes we can't help but express ourselves when there is music. Every motion can be symbolic, not necessarily of things, but of feelings. Why not express yourself to G-d with your whole body? Dance may be awkward for some of us, but done alone or in a group, it can help us unwind, to let go. We can be more open to hear and feel the Divine in our lives, in that moment.

{ 25 }

Supplication

The universe doesn't exists for us to rule it, nor be ruled by it. Yet we have free will and creative energy. The question is can G-d influence our lives and the world? Did G-d stop creating after the sixth day, or is each day something new?

It makes sense to ask for something outside our control to happen or change. Be it G-d, or Divine will, acting through us, or inspiring us, we can at least ask. Supplication is an acknowledgment that G-d matters and we want help from without. It is an acknowledgment we can't do it all ourselves. Let G-d be part of our plan.

{ 26 }

Intercession

Like supplication, intercession acknowledges G-d's place in our plans and the circumstances of the world around us. It can mean one of two things: praying on behalf of someone or asking someone to pray for you.

Some of us don't like the idea of not going directly to G-d for help, and yet we ask for prayers by those around us. Maybe we ask a departed loved one to "put in a good word" for us, in the belief that those who have passed are closer to G-d. Whatever you believe, it can't hurt to pray for others or have them pray for you. Make a point to let others know of your need. On your part, keep a prayer list of others you are praying for.

{ 27 }

Release

We've all heard, "Let go, let G-d", but do we really? We struggle with our troubles, even in our sleep.

Sometimes you have to make it clear to yourself that you can't do it all by yourself. Maybe it's out of your hands completely, but acknowledging that makes you feel helpless. Only placing it in G-d's hands -- willfully letting go -- allows the fullness of Grace to do its work. Release is a choice, then an experience. It's hard, but when we let go, we are showing our trust in Divine Providence. In the most difficult moments, we find peace.

{ 28 }

Pilgrimage

Life is a journey. A pilgrimage can be like a little life itself. You start out, seek and discover, and then return from whence you came.

Pilgrimage is a special trip devoted to a meaningful purpose. It's usually to a particular place, but it's not just about the place.

Wherever you choose, or how long you travel, it's about the journey. It's not a cruise or a vacation. You travel to feel the sense of searching and discovering. Search for G-d. Seek the Divine will. Discover G-d's answers for your questions, or even questions you didn't know to ask. The act of mindfully traveling in G-d's presence is the point. The destination can help you anticipate and open yourself up to Grace.

{ 29 }

Retreat

Sometimes you need to get away from it all. Not anywhere in particular -- you just need space. Professionals take sabbaticals, focusing on something other than the usual. But we all could use a break, to get our heads straight. Why not our hearts? A retreat is just that -- going somewhere away from everything to focus on G-d.

It's hard for most of us to take off from work and other commitments. It's hard to find somewhere free of the world's distractions. Maybe find a retreat center nearby. Maybe rent a cabin in the woods. It doesn't have to be of a particular faith, so long as you are free to have time to yourself, or be with others who are also reflecting on G-d and life.

{ 30 }

Silence

Silence can be the hardest thing in the world. We desperately want to fill the void, by listening to noise or making it ourselves. But only when we stop talking can we truly listen.

Set aside time, away from all the sounds of the outer world if you can. Let silence be a door -- hard to open and keep open at first -- by which you hear G-d's whispers. Make room for the voice of the Divine. Your own thoughts may try to pick up the slack. Know what is your own inner voice and that from G-d. And if there is no speaking at all, accept that also. Share the moment.

"Be still, and know that I am G-d."

{ 31 }

Nature

Who can look at the wonders of nature and not be moved? However you look at creation, you can see it in terms of the Divine.

Go outside. Visit the beach, the mountains, the woods. Look up at the night sky. Contemplate the beauty and endlessness of it all. See the hand of Deity. Feel blessed that you can not only experience it, but are a part of it.

{ 32 }

The Spirit

Not everyone sees G-d the same way. But most people of faith understand there is a "Spirit" or Divine Breath in the act of creation, or as an intermediary between the Unseen Creator and Creation. Some Christians call it the third personality within the Holy Trinity -- that of a helper.

If this resonates with you, focus on that aspect of G-d. Contemplate its nature. It may be the hand that takes you over the threshold from worldly things to the Kingdom of Heaven, here and in the hereafter.

{ 33 }

Existential

Does life have a purpose? Does your life have a purpose? Just asking this question can be the foundation for a conversation with G-d.

In times of crisis, we ask what we are supposed to do, or if any of it means anything. This places us in a position to stop and listen. Offer up our feelings, our unknowing, our confusion.

We cannot know all of G-d's plan for us and the world, but we can ask. What do we need to know right here and now? Accepting that it's not all up to us, and we don't have to have all the answers, is an act of faith in itself.

{ 34 }

Charity

Charity isn't just giving. Seeing G-d in others enables you to give back to G-d in a concrete, meaningful way. And it can connect you with others in a prayerful way.

When you give, truly think about those who are in need. Wish them G-d's blessing, being aware that in some small way you are doing G-d's will. And be grateful you are so blessed that you are able to do so.

{ 35 }

Communal

Communal worship isn't about conformity. Imagine an orchestra where each person plays a different instrument. Each on their own plays beautiful music, even their own unique melody. Bring them together and something amazing happens. They find a way to take their own part in something greater than themselves.

Praying together is sharing each of our relationships with G-d with each other. It's a group petition of supplication. It is the strength of cords bound together -- a heightened experience of being among others who share a lifted voice.

{ 36 }

Anger

Ever been mad at someone you Love, or someone who Loves you? Did you express that anger? Why turn away? They might be grateful that you are communicating your feelings rather than holding it in.

You could ask why bad things happen to you. It's personal. It feels unjust. You might even turn away from the very idea of Divine Existence.

If you're angry, be angry. But let G-d know you are hurting. It's not about blame, but admit the feeling of blame if you have it. Focus on how you feel, without judgment. Through sharing, the grip of anger lets go. Opening up – and lifting up – these harshest of feelings will deepen your relationship with a Loving G-d.

{ 37 }

Washing

Whether it's washing your hands or your whole body, it's not just a physical act. Cleanliness is next to G-dliness.

Using water can be an act of purity and renewal. You may wash up before a meal or at certain times of day, but it's always an opportunity for prayerfulness. If your body can be cleaner, so can your inner self. Think about those things you want to let go of for the betterment of your soul. Think about being given yet another chance. Connect the experience with G-d's desire for you to be whole and clean.

{ 38 }

Physical Love

Society often views physical love as something dirty, or base, even in a committed relationship like marriage. It's something you might want to hide from G-d, or not think about as something to share with G-d.

We are given a profound means to connect with another person, even to participate in the act of creation. Maybe we should acknowledge that as sacred in some way. Try to share all of your experiences with G-d, needs and joys, pleasure and pain. And when you share experiences with others, it's something you might be able to talk about and share with G-d together.

{ 39 }

Pride

You may think of pride as a bad thing, a vice. But is it wrong for others to be proud of you? Wouldn't you think G-d is proud of his creation?

The next time you feel pride, remember that we never truly do anything all by ourselves without Grace. But that doesn't mean we didn't accept that Grace and add it to our own free will, directing our gifts. Share with G-d that pride in yourself as part of G-d's rejoicing in a good thing.

{ 40 }

Parental

A parent's Love can be a most special thing. Our Divine Parent Loves us unconditionally. What if the roles were reversed? Could we Love G-d unconditionally, intensely holding and protecting G-d in our heart?

Christians find this in the manger, but it's an experience universal to all people. Apply those deep feelings you would have for a baby to the Divine Other. Just try it. Why keep that part of your heart out of your relationship with G-d? After all, we are called to Love as we are Loved.

{ 41 }

Blessing

What does it mean to be blessed? We may ask G-d to bless us, our meal, our home, our country. It's not just wanting all that G-d can give, but we want these things to be bless-ed, pure, holy, for the benefit of G-d's will, not just ours.

Take the time to ask blessings upon others, your work, and those things in your life you want to be put to good use.

… { 42 }

Obligatory

Sometimes you may be expected to pray. You may demand it of yourself. Maybe it's praying at a certain time and place, or for a certain reason. But that doesn't mean it has to be less meaningful.

Try not to feel guilty when prayer may seem like an obligation or a chore. You don't have to be in the mood. The important thing is setting aside the time. It's still time you spend with G-d.

{ 43 }

Resistance

When you feel least like praying, you may need it the most. It may be like hurting so much you don't want to be touched, or have anyone around you. Or maybe you are just numb. That can sometimes be worse than any pain.

Forcing ourselves is not merely a matter of discipline or courage. It is a sign that we are willing to meet G-d halfway, even when the path feels steep or even blocked. How much more might G-d appreciate that?

{ 44 }

Notes

Make your own book of personal prayer. Have a notebook or other place to jot down what prayers inspire you.

It could be other people's prayers or one's you've written yourself. You could even count your Blessings and revisit them from time to time. Just doing this opens your mind to look for ways to pray.

{ 45 }

Prayer List

Keep a list of those you pray for. Keep it somewhere you can add to it while you talk to people. And people will appreciate it if you tell them they are on your list.

Make a habit of praying through the list, perhaps before you go to sleep. Look at each person on the list and think about their need, asking G-d to be there for them.

And check in on them from time to time to see what may have changed. If the prayer has been answered, keep them on the list for a while to give thanks.

{ 46 }

Outsourcing

You can't always pray for yourself. If you are overwhelmed, or incapacitated, you might want others to pray on your behalf.

You might be hesitant to ask for help. You may not feel deserving. It's just the way some of us are. You might pray for others but feel awkward asking others to pray for you or your loved ones.

Ask anyway. Giving others the chance to pray for you isn't their burden but an opportunity -- a blessing to them and to you. Let them pray when you can't.

{ 47 }

Without Ceasing

What does it mean to pray "unceasingly"? Is it possible? We are always in the Presence of G-d, but it's hard to be aware of it in every waking moment. And what about when we sleep?

Prayerfulness is more than awareness, or an attitude. It's a place we put our hearts and minds. It goes deep, into the subconscious. The more we pray, mindfully, the more we internalize our connection with G-d's presence.

{ 48 }

...

{ Add your own way to pray here }

{ **49** }

...

{ Add your own way to pray here }

{ 50 }

...

{ Add your own way to pray here }

About the Author

Rev. Ken Stuczynski is an Interfaith Minister who works under the name Other Flock Ministries. With an educational background in Philosophy and Psychology, he is a lifelong student of scripture and world religions. Living in South Buffalo, New York with his wife and pets, he works from home as a web developer, slowly moving more toward writing and publishing.

To learn more about Ken and be on his mailing list, visit
KenVille.Net

For more information about Other Flock Ministries, visit
OtherFlock.Org

www.ingramcontent.com/pod-product-compliance
Lightning Source LLC
Chambersburg PA
CBHW052125070526
44586CB00016B/2093